It Happened to

ME

Young Offender

Interviews by Angela Neustatter and Anastasia Gonis
Photography by Laurence Cendrowicz

W

FRANKLIN WATTS
LONDON•SYDNEY

© 2004 Franklin Watts

First published in Great Britain by
Franklin Watts
96 Leonard Street
London
EC2A 4XD

Franklin Watts Australia
45-51 Huntley Street
Alexandria
NSW 2015

ISBN: 0 7496 5388 4

A CIP record for this book is available from the British Library.

Printed in Malaysia

Series editor: Sarah Peutrill
Art director: Jonathan Hair
Design: Steve Prosser
Photographs: Laurence Cendrowicz apart from pp28-33 (Matt
Hammill)

The author and publisher would especially like to thank our
interviewees and: Lee Parker, director, Youth Advocate Programme,
Brixton; Jane Chilton, RPS Rainer, Fresh Start; The authorities at
Feltham Young Offenders Institute for allowing the interview with
Steven; Steven's probation officer, Dave Freeman.

Contents

Introduction   4

Mostyn's story   6

Mostyn got into street crime when he was 16. He says he has a good family background. He has had two spells in prison.

Tania's story   12

Tania began offending after mixing with a new group of friends when she was 15. She stole from shops and was later found guilty of stealing a car and driving without a licence.

Steven's story   20

Steven is serving a sentence at Feltham Young Offenders Institute for mugging offences.

Victoria's story   28

Victoria was a drug-taker and was arrested for car-theft when she was 15.

Greg's story   34

Greg became a graffiti artist when he was 16. He had several run-ins with the police.

Tom's story   40

Tom was a victim of young offenders – he was badly beaten by a gang, and was offered no help from bystanders.

Useful addresses and contacts   46

Glossary   47

Index   48

Introduction

Why do young people offend?

Young people get into crime for all sorts of reasons, from going along with their friends, to rebellion or boredom, or even feeling that they have no other choice in life. Many, but not all, young offenders have experienced problems at home, such as family breakdown or lack of interest or support from parents.

Many people wonder why 'boredom' is cited as a reason for youth crime when the choice of activities for young people is wider than it has ever been. Some people blame the media and music culture for inciting violence.

Is youth crime a problem?

There is a general perception that youth crime is rising, but whether it is or not is disputed. Statistics show that once a young person is regularly involved in crime, they may find it difficult to break out of it altogether.

What about the law?

The age at which children become legally responsible for their actions varies in different countries. But most countries follow similar systems once a young person has been caught committing a crime. Depending on the offence they can be warned or cautioned, or fully charged. If found guilty of the offence they may be fined, given community service, a tagging order, or a custodial sentence. Most countries have separate detention centres for young people.

Real life

This book features the real-life stories of five young people who have committed crimes and one young man who was attacked by a gang of youths. The interviews are written as closely as possible from the words of the interviewee. They are written in Question and Answer format (Q and A). Alongside them you'll see some interesting facts and figures and talking points, which should help you to start thinking about some of the more complex issues. The names of some of the interviewees have been changed.

If you've been a victim of youth crime:

◆ Many people find it's good to talk about their experiences, to a friend or perhaps to a victim support group (see page 46).

If you are under pressure to commit crime:

◆ If friends are pressuring you to do something you don't want to do, ask yourself if they are real friends.
◆ Read the stories in this book. What can you learn from them?

If you are a young offender:

◆ Take a moment to examine your life. How is committing crimes affecting your life?
◆ Consider your victims: even with property crimes there are victims – someone loses out through the loss of their car, or the violation of their home.
◆ Consider the consequences if you are caught. Youth crime is not always treated lightly.

It Happened to Mostyn

Mostyn*,18, got into trouble at school. He was excluded from school and later started committing street crimes. He has been arrested five times, been in prison twice and completed a community order last year. He has not committed crimes since. He lives in London with his parents. (* Not his real name.)

Q How would you describe your family life?

A We're quite a small family, just me and my two sisters. My parents have been together throughout my childhood and they still are. My home life was and is cool. I had all that I needed at home and my parents cared for me and still do.

Q So you don't think getting into trouble with the law had anything to do with the way things were in your childhood?

A I absolutely don't think so. I didn't have bad experiences like some kids do. They seem to react against their lives being so tough by going wrong. With me, crime was just what I chose to do. There were no reasons I can point to that justify it.

Q Did you get on well at school?

A School was fine in the sense that I did quite well with my studies, but I started getting into fights when I was ten. I was seen as a troublemaker. But it was as much due to the other guys I fought with. I think we were just being boisterous. I was suspended a couple of times and then I was kicked out.

Q How did you feel about the school's reaction?

A I don't know whether it was race or just that they'd identified me as a troublemaker, but it seemed to me the teachers were always watching me, always on my back. It made me angry and of course that made them recognise me even more.

Q What did your parents feel about you getting into trouble?

A They weren't particularly happy, but they felt better when I started secondary school because I did fine at first and was appreciating learning things. I had lots of friends from the area - there were strong friendship bonds.

Q But things didn't stay that good?

A No. I got into a scrap on the bus and pushed the

It's a Fact that...

The proportion of the population in England and Wales of black ethnic origin is estimated to be 2 per cent, black or black British. However black young people account for 6.1 per cent of the population sentenced through the youth justice system.

person I was tussling with off. He was quite badly hurt. So I got excluded from school for that.

Q Didn't that upset your parents?

A Of course, but my dad had decided to take us all to Jamaica, where he comes from. We went for three years. I was in school there and didn't get into trouble. By the time I returned to the UK I had several exams equivalent to good GCSEs but, unfortunately, they are not recognised over here.

Q How old were you when you arrived back?

A I was 16 and I didn't want to go to school again, but none of the careers on offer seemed at all stimulating. This was 2000

and my friends were out of school and all doing street crime and making money. So I joined them and spent all day committing crimes to get goods to sell. I won't say my friends were a bad influence because I make my own decisions about what I do. I chose to go with them.

> "I won't say my friends were a bad influence ... I chose to go with them."

Q Were your parents aware of what you were doing during the day?

A They were both at work all day and didn't know how I spent my time. I think they must have wondered how I managed to come home with new trainers and things. Thinking about it now I suppose they must have worried a bit. But if they'd really realised what I was up to, I'm sure they would have found a way to stop me.

> " [My parents] were both at work all day and didn't know how I spent my time."

Q So when did they find out?

A When I got arrested for street robbery. I was very upset the first time, worried about what my family would think. None of them are criminals. They came to court with me and I got a supervision order. My parents were angry and upset because they never brought me up that way.

Q What did you have to do under the supervision order?

A I had to go and see my Youth Offending Team (YOT) worker regularly. His job was to make sure I was in education or some occupation to keep me off the streets. I also had to spend time at a community

project in Streatham and do woodwork. The YOT team - it's several people involved with your case - talked about what they could do to help me stop crime, but frankly I thought it a waste of time. It didn't mean anything to me.

Q But did you stop committing crime?

A Not at all. Through the time of the order, as well as afterwards, I just carried on with thieving. I didn't feel bad about it. I just saw it as a way of making money.

Q Weren't you worried about getting arrested again?

A Not particularly. The chances of getting caught are actually very low. You keep

It's a Fact that....

In a US survey:
◆ 87 per cent of people wanted adult sentences for young people who committed serious violent crimes
◆ 69 per cent wanted adult sentences for drug sellers
◆ 63 per cent wanted adult sentences for young people charged with serious property offences.

doing things and you calculate there's a chance of being caught, but there's a good chance you won't.

Q So did you get away with it after that?

A No, I didn't. The police picked me up again. It was about three months after the last time. This time it was for a smash-and-grab raid. I was put on another YOT order but, I'll be honest, it made no difference. I kept on doing the same things.

Q Did you think being black made things more difficult for you?

A Not more difficult in life generally but I do think the police arrested me and other blacks more than whites.

Q You got arrested again, for street crimes, didn't you?

A Yes, and I was frightened this time that I'd get sent down. I'd heard about prison from people. They had some nasty tales but they regarded it as an occupational hazard. They weren't about to give up crime because they didn't

know a way to make that much money, so they accepted they might have to spend some time inside. I was sent to a youth prison and I was scared, man, and that lasted for the first few days. But then I settled and worked out the system. Being shut up with too much time to think, the fear of bullying, being treated by some as scum isn't nice. And I missed my family. I didn't want to be there, but I had a 13-month sentence to serve.

Q Did anyone try to help you?

A Yes, a lot of people tried. But I didn't want advice on

"I'd heard about prison from people. They had some nasty tales but they regarded it as an occupational hazard... they accepted they might have to spend some time inside."

> **"I also had to do an offending behaviour programme which gets you to look at what living life as a criminal really means."**

how to change. Prison isn't a place that makes you feel like taking advice. I didn't want to stop crime. The only thing was I knew it made my parents unhappy.

Q And you did get into trouble again?

A The last time I was arrested was for a driving offence. Because I'd been in prison they wouldn't give me bail so I was sent back to prison for several weeks on remand. But when I went to court to be sentenced they

decided I didn't need to go back to prison as I'd spent time there. So they gave me an Intensive Surveillance and Supervision Programme. It's another community order but it's a lot tougher than the ones I had earlier. On this, I had an advocate who spent several hours a day monitoring me. He also tried to build trust and help me to see there could be a better way to live life.

Q How was that for you?

A Because I wasn't locked up and feeling angry I did listen. In a way what he said I knew already, but I liked my advocate and my order was supervised by the Youth Advocate Programme in Brixton and there are good people there. You feel they really are looking out for you.

Q What did your advocate do with you during the time you spent together?

A He took me to the gym, to the cinema and places like that. I also had to do an offending behaviour programme which gets you to look at what living life as a criminal really means. You also explore the effect crime has on victims. My advocate sorted out other courses: I did one on football coaching. I did a lifeguard course and a weights instructor course. I did an entry into youth work course and some volunteer work on a youth project.

Q So are you interested in doing any of those as a job?

A I am quite interested in youth work. I feel I could be quite good because if youngsters were getting into trouble, I'd know what was going on and I might be able to help.

Q It sounds as though you got quite a lot out of your programme, but did it change your offending behaviour?

A Yes, it did. I decided it wasn't worth it - there are better ways to live. I don't want to spend years of my life in jail, and obviously that could happen the way I was going on. Also I feel, through the Centre, that there are people who care about me who will support me when I need it.

Q What about your friends?

A They are still in crime and getting jail sentences. I can see that I'm bright enough to do things in life that will make money and I can have fun and be free.

Q So this had more effect than your prison sentence?

A Yes, I think getting a chance to work things out with intensive support in the community was really good for me. My advocate helped me see that my family don't need the grief I've been giving them. I know it stresses them and I've got

" I'm big now, not a silly little kid."

little cousins who look up to me. I want them to be able to go on doing that.

Q So do you feel crime is in the past now?

A I don't think I'll go back into crime. I don't need to be on the streets as I was, which is where it was all happening. I'm big now, not a silly little kid. ∎

Talking Points

◆ Mostyn says his friends did not lead him into crime. Do you think this is likely to be true? How big an influence are friends generally?

◆ Statistically prison sentences don't act as a deterrent when people come out of prison. Why do you think this is? What do you think the main reason for prisons is – to reform criminals, to protect others, or to act simply as a punishment?

It Happened to Tania

Tania, 22, grew up in Dorset, UK. She first got into trouble with the police when she was 15 and she was put on probation after her third offence of taking and driving away a car without insurance. She was referred to the Rainer Fresh Start project. She now lives with her partner and baby son, Jake. Here she tells her story and Fresh Start caseworker, Jane Chilton, explains the project's work to help Tania take charge of her life and stop offending.

Q Did you grow up with both your parents?

A No. My mum left when I was 18 months old and my dad and nan brought me up.

Q How do you think your mum going affected you?

A It was really difficult not having a mother because all my friends had theirs and I felt the odd one out. At least I had a dad while lots of my friends didn't.

Q Did you ever think of trying to find her?

A All through my childhood I tried to find my mum but all my efforts reached a dead end. Nobody seemed willing to help me really. But now I think that may have been a good thing - I had a better life not living with her because she ended up with a man who beat her up. I found that out in my teens.

Q So was it just you and your father at home?

A When I was 12 my father remarried. At first I didn't

get on with my stepmother and I think I made things quite hard for her. But she tried hard and treated me like her own and I began to see that she was on my side and cared for me. In fact when my dad was being hard on me she would stick up for me.

Q So life improved after that?

A Well it changed. My dad brought me up very strictly and when he remarried he

First Offences

When young people first get into trouble, behave anti-socially or commit minor offences, they can often be dealt with outside the court system. The purpose of these pre-court orders is to stop young people getting into the Youth Justice System too early, while still offering them the help and support they need to stop offending. Systems are different throughout the world but here are some examples:

◆ Acceptable Behaviour Contract or Bond: a young person agrees to stop the behaviour that causes a nuisance to the local community and takes part in activities to address their behaviour.

◆ Anti-Social Behaviour Orders: a young person is not allowed to go to particular places or do particular things.

◆ Curfew: a young person must be at home by a certain time in the evening.

◆ Child Safety Orders: a social worker supervises the child.

◆ Reprimand: a formal verbal warning is given by a police officer to a young person who admits they are guilty of a minor first offence. If the offence is repeated it might lead to a final warning.

loosened up on me, so then I decided to run wild. I felt I could do things I wanted now. All my mates were going out on Friday nights and getting drunk so I started joining up with them. I bunked off from school. I did pass my exams but not with very good grades.

> **"The police would come to look for us, take us to the police station and call the children's home to get us. It was like a game to us."**

Q Did running wild get you into trouble at home?

A My dad and I bickered and argued quite a lot and he was angry with me quite

often. So after one row, when I was 15, I ran away. I decided I wanted something different. I had a mate living in a children's home, which sounded good, so I got social services to place me there.

Q Was that a good decision?

A I made a lot of friends, but they were people my parents wouldn't have been happy about. Most had quite bad backgrounds and had been in trouble, but I found them fun and amusing. I wanted to belong with them.

Q What did belonging mean?

A I started joining them: getting into trouble, runing away to the sea-front at Weymouth to hang out. The police would come to look for us, take us to the police station and call the children's

home to get us. It was like a game to us.

Q Was that the worst you did?

A No. I was drinking quite a lot at this time and I was angry a lot. At the children's home several of us had a row with one of the boys living in a home close by. We went to his place and smashed a door to get at him. I had been drinking at the time. The police arrested us and we spent the night in the cells at the station. The next morning we were taken to court and given a caution.

Q Did you feel frightened by that?

A No. I didn't see it as the beginning of getting into a lifestyle of being in trouble with the law. I didn't see any reason to change the way I was behaving. Nobody else at the home was stopped by cautions.

Q So you went on doing things that got you into trouble with the law?

A I spent about ten months at the home. During that time I was getting into

It's a Fact that...

Girls accounted for 23.5 per cent of youth offenders in 2000 in England and Wales, a rise from 20.3 per cent in 1991. In Western Australia 19 per cent of youth offenders are female.

It's a Fact that...

During the 1990s in England and Wales the number of cautions for young people declined sharply, resulting in a larger proportion being prosecuted and, as a result, receiving a criminal record.

> " I knew what I was doing was wrong ... but it was how I wanted to be. I really didn't consider any consequences."

trouble at least once a month, sometimes just for underage drinking, and I was truanting from school when I had a hangover. But one time I lost my temper after a row with a girl at the home. I was charged for that and taken to court. They bound me over to keep the peace and fined me – they took that out of my pocket money at the home. I knew what I was doing was wrong and that not everybody out there was like that, but it was how I wanted to be. I really didn't consider any consequences.

Q Did you stay at the children's home?

A No. I was beginning to miss my family and they had always made it plain I could go home, so I did. I was 17 by this time and it was here that I got into trouble with my temper again. There was a girl who lived two doors from us and she had been picking on my brother. So one night when she came up to me in Weymouth, and I had been drinking, I smashed her in the face. The police came and arrested me at my dad's house.

It's a Fact that...

A survey of school children in 2001 in the UK found that 43.9 per cent of boys and 37.4 per cent of girls aged 16 have stolen items in the past.

Q How did your father react?

A He was very cross and said he couldn't believe I could be so stupid. I was worried this time because, living with my parents, I didn't want to cause them trouble. But they never sat me down and talked to me about what I was doing. My dad took the view I had to learn from my mistakes and the consequences.

Q Did you settle down then, living at home?

A I did a bit, but then my parents decided to move to Worthing. I went with them, but I missed everyone in Dorset so I went back. I got a bed-sit and lived on income support. I started to mix with people I would avoid now, but then they seemed like friends. I couldn't see they were leading me into trouble again.

Q What did that mean this time?

A We were stealing from shops. Mostly razor blades and packets of bacon because we could easily sell those. One of us would go in and pinch the stuff and the other would keep watch. It didn't seem wrong to me. We weren't hurting anyone and they could get it back off the insurance. I wouldn't burgle someone's home.

Q So when was the next time you were arrested?

A That was for something different. My boyfriend had nicked a car and I persuaded him to let me drive it. But when I put it into gear it jerked backwards and I hit a bloke on a moped and knocked him off. I thought I'd hurt him badly and I was scared. I thought of doing a runner but I knew you got twice the punishment for a hit-and-run offence.

Q What happened this time?

A I was arrested and given a solicitor. I knew this was more serious than the times before. I went to court and was given bail but it was only about a week to the next hearing. This time I really panicked because my solicitor said, 'When you go to court take a bag with your things, because there's a high chance you won't be leaving again.' I realised then that I could lose my freedom and go to prison.

> " ... they seemed like friends. I couldn't see they were leading me into trouble again."

Q So did that happen?

A I was found guilty of taking and driving away and not having a licence. When the magistrates came into court I heard them say, 'custodial sentence' and I was terrified. I wondered for a moment if I could do a runner. But then they started talking to me and said they were giving me probation, fining me and I was banned from driving for a year. I thought I was really lucky. But this time I had decided I had to stop getting into trouble.

Q How easy was that going to be?

A I'd moved to Worthing to my family home, but there really wasn't room for me and they wanted me out. I think that was why the court referred me to Fresh Start, a project which gives you a place to live and lots of support. I was lucky to get my caseworker, Jane Chilton.

Q Jane, why was Tania referred to you?

A (J) Everyone referred to us is an ex-offender and they

" ... when I put [the car] into gear it jerked backwards and I hit a bloke on a moped and knocked him off. I thought I'd hurt him badly and I was scared. "

"I met my partner on the Fresh Start project and we've got a baby, Jake..."

come through the probation service. We run a programme called Fresh Start which is for young people who are vulnerable and in need of some help to get their lives straight. So we have a shared house and flats which they get for a fixed period. We have regular meetings with them where we discuss home circumstances, substance abuse, health, relationships, and we try to explore with them what led to offending. It's also a chance for the young people to tell us their side of things.

It's a Fact that...

Poor achievement or lack of interest in school and a history of problems at home in the family are linked to a higher chance of a young person being involved in crime.

Q Did you see things in Tania's background that may have made her vulnerable to getting into trouble?

A (J) She didn't get as much nurturing as would have been desirable and I would say hers was a difficult family background. She saw the group she got into trouble with as role models and they accepted her and seemed to want her around, so that was quite seductive.

Q Tania, what happened when you went to Fresh Start?

A I had a room in a shared house and I felt good with

that. I was supposed to go to group sessions with other people on the project but they were mostly boys and I didn't feel happy there. I met with Jane at the office a lot and that was good because it helped me make a routine for the day. She would ask me how I was doing, how she could help, and we would discuss my problems. But she was also very clear - I wouldn't be kept on the project if I got into trouble again.

Q Jane, what did you see as the most pressing issues for Tania?

A (J) Apart from needing somewhere to live, Tania needed help with employment and training so that she could get skills for working at something she wanted, and she needed to establish stability in her life. One of the main things we had to work on was anger management because her explosive anger was the biggest cause of her getting into trouble.

Q Did this all go smoothly?

A I haven't offended for five years. I met my partner on the Fresh Start project and we've got a baby, Jake, so I'm not working but I might go to college in the future. Jane has helped me with advice and really taken an interest in the baby.

Q Jane, how much has Tania changed since joining Fresh Start?

A (J) Once we started anger management work she would ring me or come and see me to talk things through rather than letting her anger loose. That way we have been able to look at different ways to deal with the situation and get a positive outcome. Tania has got a lot of grit and determination and is very good at organising things these days. It's two years since she finished with the project but she still comes in with the baby and is very keen to make things work in her life. I count her as a success.

Q Tania, what difference has Fresh Start made to you?

A I've been helped to see how I can control myself and make my life work. I've no doubt that having support helps me stay out of trouble. ■

Talking Points

◆ Tania says she and her friends stole from shops. This did not seem wrong to her as it did not hurt anyone and the shops could claim from their insurance. Do you agree with her?

◆ Tania was never given a custodial sentence for her offences, despite committing some serious crimes. Do you think she should have been given a prison sentence?

◆ Projects like Fresh Start are very expensive to run, and usually have to be funded by the tax-payer. Do you think they are worthwhile?

It Happened to Steven

Steven, 15, first started committing crimes aged 11. He has had been given warnings, several probation orders and has twice been held in secure units. He is now serving a sentence in Feltham Young Offenders Institute. He has three siblings and one of his elder brothers is also in prison.

Q Did you get into trouble from a young age?

A No I wasn't in trouble at all until I was nine. Then my mum passed away and it hurt badly, but I couldn't do anything about it and I didn't think I should cry.

Q Did your dad help you?

A He's always been there for me but it was tough for him too and we both just had to get on with it.

Q Did things change for you after this?

A I stopped going to school when I was 11. I used to go every day but things were hurting too much. I couldn't hack it any more. There didn't seem to be anyone who understood and I just wasn't coping with being at school.

Q So what did you do with your time then?

A I started mixing with people who were hanging out on the estate where I lived and on the street. They were the wrong people to mix with, I can see now, because they were doing crime.

Q So did you start doing crime too?

A Not at first. I just hung about with them but then they started urging me to join in so I did. We were breaking into cars, stealing stereos then going and selling them.

Q Did you feel bad or worried about what you were doing?

A I didn't feel bad but I was scared of being caught.

> " I stopped going to school when I was 11. I used to go every day but things were hurting too much. I couldn't hack it any more. "

Court

If a young person commits a serious offence, or offends several times, they may have to go to court to be tried. Court systems are different around the world, but here are the basics of what would happen in most cases.

Bail - If the case cannot be dealt with immediately, the court will make a decision as to whether the young person will be bailed (allowed to stay at home, usually subject to some conditions) or remanded into custody (imprisoned until the case goes to court).

Solicitors - An offender will have a solicitor who represents them in court and acts independently, in their best interest. They work for the defender, not their parents or other professionals. The solicitor takes instructions from the young person and provides them with legal advice on the charge, procedure and plea (guilty or not guilty). They also speak for the young person in the court.

The trial - When it comes to trial, if a young person pleads not guilty a date will be set for the trial when the evidence will be heard, and a judge or a jury will decide whether or not they are guilty. If the decision is guilty, they will then decide on the most appropriate sentence, based on the country's laws

Youth courts - In some countries young offenders are dealt with by youth courts. These usually deal with people under the age of 18, and usually cannot sentence offenders to long prison sentences. They tend to be less formal than adult courts.

> ## "I had never expected to get into crime but at this time I saw it as the only way I could manage."

Q Did you remain scared of getting caught?

A No. After a while, I got used to it because we were doing it all day long. I became quite bold. I felt happy with these people; they really accepted me and I had money in my hands. I had never expected to get into crime but at this time I saw it as the only way I could manage.

It's a Fact that...

In Britain more than 14,000 18- to 20-year-olds are jailed each year.

Q When were you first arrested?

A I was 13 at the time and I was breaking into a car when a police car pulled up. These coppers came out and they handcuffed me. I was frightened then because I'd never been arrested before and I had no idea what would happen. I thought they would take me straight away to a juvenile jail.

Q How did your father react?

A Dad had no idea what I was up to until my arrest and he was angry with me. He said, 'If you need money why didn't you come to me?' But I didn't want to ask him for money.

Q What happened to you?

A I was given a warning and the police told me how serious it was to be getting into crime. They said, although they weren't charging me this time, that was the way I was going.

Q You were only 13 at this time. Did anyone try to get you back into school?

A The education people did try but I'd promise to go and then just not turn up. I know that sometimes the social services get involved when you don't go to school but they didn't with me.

Q Did your father try to make sure you didn't get into trouble again?

A He tried to ground me but it didn't work. When I begged him to let me go out he did and then I just met up with my friends again. Once I was with them I was breaking into cars again.

Q Were you caught this time?

A Not immediately but apparently I was seen and a week later there was a knock on the door at

6 a.m. I was in bed and Dad insisted on waking me. He didn't let the police up to my room, but he just said come downstairs and didn't tell me why. So as I came downstairs I saw these three officers and knew I had to go with them.

Q Now were you scared?

A Not as much as the time before and they just gave me another warning. You get three warnings before they lock you up, but the third one is when you are charged.

Q So did you stop then?

A No. I didn't and next time I was arrested they took me to court and I was given six months' probation. I didn't know what it meant when the judge said it so my solicitor had to explain to me. I went twice a week to this guy, Dave Freeman. He explained that I was going down the wrong road, I'd end up inside and he talked about how my crimes hurt people. I listened and it impressed me at the time, but as soon as I left Dave I forgot.

Q Was your dad involved in your probation?

A He didn't come to the meetings but I think Dave may have talked to him about keeping me away from my friends because he gave me odd jobs and kept me busy almost all the time.

Q Did that help you avoid crime?

A I went the whole six months of my probation

> **"I was arrested they took me to court and I was given six months probation."**

> **"When you are committing crimes it's exciting, you get a charge and then if someone comes you just run. It's a bit like a game."**

without getting into trouble but two days after it finished I was back with the crowd again. I knew if I broke my probation by doing crime I'd get a stiff punishment.

Q Were you committing the same crimes?

A No. My mates had moved up a level and now they were stealing cars and driving them - twocking [taking without consent].

Q How did you feel when you committed these crimes?

A When you are committing crimes it's exciting, you get a charge and then if someone comes you just run. It's a bit like a game. We did it at night at first but then we got bolder and did it in broad daylight too. We drove the cars until the petrol ran out and left them. But we got too mad - we were taking five or six cars a night. I didn't sleep much at that time.

Q And you got caught then?

A I did and I was given another two months' probation and this time they put me on a course for motor mechanics because I was interested in that. But it started too early in the morning and I didn't go. My dad said I should go back to school but I didn't want to do that. So of course I had all that free time and I started shoplifting as well as doing the cars. I was given a conditional discharge but I broke that and the next time I was caught twocking the courts said I had been given enough chances. They sent me to a secure unit.

Q How did you feel when you heard you would be locked-up?

A This time I was really frightened because I imagined a really tough place with 24-hour bang-up, but in fact we were all children and out of our rooms most of the time. And there was a member of staff for every lad who tried to help you sort out problems and set up a plan for when you got out so you didn't get into trouble again.

Q Did this sentence make any difference?

A I was in prison for six months and I stayed out of trouble for six months afterwards, but one day one of my friends knocked on the door and I was back to crime but this time it was

> **"The first boy I mugged looked at me and I felt sorry for him so I backed off."**

It's a Fact that...

Prison probably does not stop young people from returning to crime: 75 per cent of 18- to 24-year-olds remanded in prison in the UK go on to re-offend.

worse because we were doing street robbery - mugging.

Q Did that feel different to taking cars and stealing goods?

A I didn't feel so good about this, although I never used a knife. I used to go with one other person and we used threats. The first boy I mugged looked at me and I felt sorry for him so I backed off. In fact the only people I could rob were the ones who didn't look at me but I stopped feeling bad about doing it.

Q Did you ever think how it would feel it if were you?

A I never thought about that and in due course I was picked up and sent away again. I went to two more secure units and a secure training centre. But one day

I was told to pack up my stuff because I was going to Feltham Young Offenders Institute. I'd heard a lot of bad stories so I was really scared this time and I realised there was nothing I could do.

" I'd heard a lot of bad stories so I was really scared this time and I realised there was nothing I could do."

25

"I know I have to avoid my old friends but that's really hard where I live..."

26

Q Is it as bad as you feared?

A Not that bad because I haven't been bullied and I've got used to the regime. But there are officers who act like tough guys and I just want to be with my family. I don't want to spend my life in and out of prison, but I can see this is what will happen if I don't stop getting into trouble. Dave has told me very clearly that if I'm arrested again I'll get a much longer sentence. I've seen it with my older brother who is in prison for longer. I listen to what Dave says because I feel he understands me. Not like most adults.

Q So how will you stop?

A I know I have to avoid my old friends but that's really hard where I live because there's nothing to do on the estate or in the area and everyone just hangs around. But my dad really wants to help. He's a mechanic and says he'll give me work if he's got enough. I'm good at painting and decorating and bricklaying so Dave may help me get a job in that.

Q Is there anything else that will help you try not to get back into trouble?

A I've got a younger brother of eleven. He looks up to me and I don't want him turning out like I have. If I stop committing crimes then he's not going to see me doing it and follow my example. ■

" I've got a younger brother ... I don't want him turning out like I have."

Talking Points

◆ Steven was given a custodial sentence after three warnings – a 'three strikes and you're out' policy. Is this a good policy do you think? Did it act as a deterrent for Steven?

◆ Steven isn't the only one in his family who has committed crimes, and he is also concerned about his younger brother. Do you think having a sibling who has committed crimes is a bad influence? Do you think friends or siblings are greater influences?

◆ Steven finds it harder to commit mugging crimes because then he has to face his victim. Car theft still involves a victim. Do you think offenders generally consider this? Is it more acceptable if it's an insurance company that has to pay?

27

It Happened to Victoria

Victoria, 17, is unemployed and lives with her mother in Melbourne, Australia. She was a drug-taker and was arrested for car theft when she was 15.

Q Why did you commit the offence?

A Well, I was using a lot of speed every day, injecting amphetamines, and I wasn't thinking straight. So I committed a bad crime.

Q How did the drug-taking start?

A Well, from the age of 13 to 15, I'd had very bad experiences with boyfriends. Then there was one incident with my father - something that I'd rather not talk about. It did affect me in a big way, and I started taking drugs, which led me to the crime - I was with my boyfriend and we stole a car together.

Q What happened when you took the car?

A It was my boyfriend who said, 'Let's do it!' I wasn't thinking right from all the drugs, so I just went with him. I didn't know what I was doing. The police only found me in the car and I got charged with the whole offence. My boyfriend just let me be done for the whole charge.

"I didn't know what I was doing."

Q Had your then boyfriend any history of offences before?

A He had been charged with car theft several times, and with robbery from stores and lots of other places. He had a long list of offences, but I had not taken part in any of them before the car theft.

Q How were you punished for the car theft?

A I was put on a good behaviour bond. Then I broke that, so I had to go back to court.

Q What were the repercussions of that?

A I was sent to the Children's Court Clinic. A child-psychiatrist assessed me and then part of the bail agreement was that I keep seeing her.

Q Do you find that talking to the counsellor is a help?

A Not always. She talks as if she knows everything about me, and I don't like that because she doesn't. It makes me feel uncomfortable. Sometimes it does help, but not always. She made me talk about what I have done. Sometimes this made me more anxious and it often led me to further drug use and self-mutilation. I ended up having a seizure as a result of all the stress - I am an epileptic.

Q Do you still see a counsellor?

A Yes, several times a week. For instance, today I did not go into school because I was feeling too stressed. I get stressed when I cannot meet my school assignment deadlines. I spoke to my counsellor several times throughout the day. She tried to talk to me about the stress because I wasn't attending school.

Q How did the offence influence your immediate family?

A I live with my mother. It hurt her very much, particularly seeing me using drugs.

Q What effect did that have on you?

A I decided to go cold turkey. It took me three months, but I managed to stop injecting drugs. I have been off them totally for a year now.

It's a Fact that...

Young offenders are more likely to have taken cannabis (56 per cent) or heroin (13 per cent) than those who have never committed a non-drug-related offence (13 per cent and 1 per cent respectively).

29

Q What about your friends? What did they think?

A Well, they just thought that I was an idiot for becoming so badly involved with drugs. They thought that I wasn't worth anything. Now I don't have any friends at all. I can't make friends. I don't mix well with others.

Q What happened at school?

A I actually missed a year, because of the epilepsy. I went right off the rails. I was unable to concentrate or study. I lost interest in everything because of the stress I was going through.

> " Now, I don't have any friends at all. I can't make friends. I don't mix well with others. "

Q Did you do anything instead?

A I knew I had to do something because I was going a bit nuts not doing anything, so I did a retail course. I enjoyed doing that course. It took about three months, and I passed the course.

Q Do you think that helped you focus a little bit more?

A Yes, for sure.

Q Did you go back to that school?

A No. My old school kicked me out because of the drug use. So, that made me ask, 'What am I doing?' I really liked that school. It was wonderful there. Now they've sent me to a school where all the kids have problems, so, it's pretty much up to me. That's what it all comes down to.

Q Are you enjoying school now?

A I have my good days and bad days.

Q What type of teachers do you have at your present school?

A They're all pretty good. They're friendly and encouraging. They make sure that I am always on track. If they see you don't come in for a few days, or see that you are not yourself, they are very kind. When my father passed away, they were very understanding of my situation and attitude. Things like that are taken into consideration. They're very good that way.

Q Who has helped you the most since the offence?

A My mum supports me. Whenever I need her she's always there. I also met my current boyfriend, Carlos, three months ago, and we have joined a Christian church youth group and we go there together. They are very supportive and they have dancing and music nights for young people. They help us to enjoy ourselves and these meetings teach me to mix with others. I don't have much contact with other people. So, I like going there. I'm learning to have faith.

Q Had you had any contact with religion before this?

A I used to go to a church every week with my

mother and brother when I was young. Afterwards we'd have dinner at the Reverend's house. It was great. I enjoyed it very much. I liked going there. That was when I was quite young. But I have happy memories of that time.

Q Apart from giving up drugs, did you want to make any other changes to make life better for yourself?

A Yes. I had to stop having so much fun, I suppose.

Q Is this how you see having fun?

A No, not now I don't, but it was fun at the time.

Q Do you think you could or would, offend again?

A No. Well, not the same offence, anyway.

Q What do you hope for in the future?

A I'm working towards passing my exams.

It's a Fact that...

In Western Australia 41 per cent of young offenders are given non-custodial sentences, while 31 per cent are fined. Only 13 per cent are put into custody.

Q Have you set any long-term goals for yourself since you stopped taking drugs?

A Yes and no. Because I have epilepsy, that limits me a great deal in the sort of jobs I can choose from. I know I want to travel. I might go travelling for a year or something like that, just like my sister did. She had a break from study and then went back to Uni. She's doing very well at it.

> " Young people don't understand the effect one single act can have. They do something and it's too late. "

Q What would you say to someone who thought that stealing a car is a good idea?

A There are lots of kids that I would like to take into my experience, into my life. I would show them all the repercussions that drug use can have: the involvement with the law and everything that happens when you commit an offence. Young people don't understand the effect one single act can have. They do something and it's too late.

Q Do you feel that your experiences have given you a new direction in life?

A Yes, I know they have. I think I might like to become a psychologist. I would like to help people who have had problems. I will be able to understand them because of my personal experiences and show them how they can change. Unlike a psychologist who has learned what they know from books, I have gone through all the hell of experiencing things myself. ■

Talking Points

◆ Victoria blames her offence on drug-taking. Do you think this is a valid excuse? What about the other problems she's experienced in her life – should these be taken into account?

◆ Is car-theft a victimless crime? Do you think Victoria's punishment was appropriate? Do you feel she has remorse for what she's done?

◆ Why do you think the court recommended a counsellor for Victoria? What effect has the counsellor had? Should every offender have counselling?

It Happened to Greg

Greg*, 23, a university graduate, became a graffiti artist in his teens. Doing graffiti in illegal places got him into trouble with the police. He lives in Manchester.
(* Not his real name.)

Q How would you describe your childhood?

A I come from a single-parent family but that hasn't been a problem. My mum has coped well with me and my brother and I would describe it as a happy, middle-class family life with a stable home.

Q What was your experience of school?

A I went to a great primary school and made good friends. I also enjoyed the different experiences. I still have the friends I made in secondary school. But I went to a tutorial college from 16 because I wasn't settling down to work - I was having a good time and rebelling against schoolwork. At first I didn't like the idea of tutorial college but in the end I enjoyed the rigorous teaching and made some different friends there. So overall the school years were a good time for me.

Q Were you in a rebellious frame of mind during your later teens?

A I wouldn't put it quite like that. My mother is a

person who tries to be on the side of her children and we talked a lot about things. I could always express my views so I didn't have much to rebel against. But I suppose I've always been a bit against the grain.

Q What led you into doing graffiti?

A I got involved with hip hop culture which was big with the young at that time. Graffiti wasn't really so popular at that time so my friends and I came to it spontaneously as an exciting way of expressing ourselves artistically. It started because several of us enjoyed drawing

> " ... my friends and I came to it spontaneously as an exciting way of expressing ourselves artistically."

It's a Fact that...

In a survey on crime and anti-social behaviour in England and Wales, people said they feared graffiti and other vandalism to property more than any other kind of local community disorder crime. This included noisy neighbours, drug-dealing, and being attacked because of colour.

together. We would draw in a room, on paper, practising outlines and so on. But then we wanted to take it further.

Q So what did that mean?

A We wanted to make it part of the environment.

Q Did you find public places where graffiti was permitted?

A There was a big walled area in the middle of town and people came from all over Europe to make graffiti on it. It was very exciting, a kind of constantly changing art exhibition. I used to hang out there and meet other people.

Q What effect did this have on you?

A I saw graffiti as a really important and inspiring way of creating art and I knew I wanted to do the kind of big, beautiful murals that were being created.

Q What happened then?

A The local authorities closed the space where we did graffiti and I really don't know why. It was a disused place and we weren't doing any harm - I'd say we were contributing something original and different. Suddenly all the kids who went there at weekends and expressed themselves

35

> **" We found abandoned bits of land, old buildings and so on. We didn't see any harm in this."**

through art had nowhere to go. I know some that then started to go to illegal places like the train tracks.

Q **So where did you go to do graffiti?**

A I was 17 at the time and in sixth form college working for A' levels. I was doing graffiti in my spare time with a couple of friends. We found abandoned bits of land, old buildings and so on. We didn't see any harm in this.

Q **What happened when you had done you're A' levels?**

A I got the grades I needed for university and I took up a place that autumn.

Q **So did you forget about graffiti then?**

A In fact it was at university that I met a student who had done some really impressive graffiti which excited me a lot. He helped me to learn to paint much better, to develop new colour techniques. And I started to look more closely at the graffiti that had become popular at this time. Travelling around England I saw some mind-blowing walls and I realised what a lot it was possible to do with graffiti.

> **"...I saw some mind-blowing walls and I realised what a lot it was possible to do with graffiti."**

It's a Fact that...

In the UK millions of pounds are spent on cleaning up graffiti. In 2003 the British Prime Minister listed graffiti as a symptom of 21st-century life with drug-pushers and hooligans.

Q When you went out to do graffiti, was it in illegal places?

A Yes, if I couldn't find anywhere legal. For instance before the Iraq war I saw a big green board on a site visible to people on passing trains. I wrote a big 'No War' statement. I often went out pretty late and I would go on to the train track after the trains had stopped running. You've got big areas of wall and there's a very quiet, strange atmosphere.

Q Did you ever worry about being caught?

A I knew I wasn't allowed to be there so I was always bothered about being seen. I absolutely didn't want to get caught.

Q So did you get caught?

A Yes, but not on the railway tracks. One time I was a bit drunk and I went into an old building in town. The place was due to be knocked down so I went inside and painted on the walls. I wanted to photograph what I had done so I went outside to go home and get my camera. It was then I realised there was a police car parked there. It hit me then that I was in trouble and I remember feeling frightened and panicky.

Q What happened?

A These two police officers took me in the car to the police station. Then I had to sit there waiting to be dealt with. I was sobering up by this time and suddenly I was very aware of being in a big institution, and knowing there was nothing I could do to get out of the trouble I was in. I had to give my name and address and I was booked in. A police officer asked me questions like, 'Why did you do it?' One officer asked if I had a pathological impulse to do graffiti!

Q Did they tell you your rights?

A Yes.

Q What was your attitude to the police and what was happening?

A I decided the best thing was to be well-mannered and co-operative. So I apologised for what I had done and tried to do and say what the police wanted. I do think it made things better than if I'd been swearing.

Q What was their attitude to you?

A I felt they were trying to work out what sort of person I was and if I was likely to be committing other crimes. And I think they wanted me to have a fright. They put me in a cell

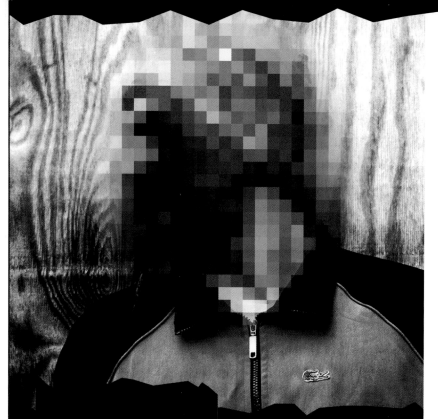

> " ... and I realised how it would feel to be inside, absolutely powerless and at the mercy of the system."

for a few hours. That was horrible and I realised how it would feel to be inside, absolutely powerless and at the mercy of the system.

Q Did the police charge you?

A No. When they let me out they said I must come back a month later. I felt very worried during that time, not knowing what would happen when I went back. In fact they told me they were taking no further action, and they gave me a caution which is basically pointing out that you are breaking the law and that the punishment could be worse next time.

Q So did you stop doing graffiti then?

A No. Even though I'd been frightened, I wasn't careful enough. It was on New Year's Eve. I was five minutes from home and I saw a big advertising billboard and some black boards underneath it. So I sprayed my name there - I've always felt putting my name on corporate boards is a good thing to do. But the next minute I was collared by a police officer.

Q Were you on your own?

A No. I was with my girlfriend and they took us both to the police station. We were huddled together in the back of the car and I thought, 'This is it. I'm in big trouble now.'

Q How did the police treat you?

A Not bad. Interacting with them changed my view a bit. I saw that some are bastards but some are okay. What I didn't like was that they took a DNA swab from my cheek, and that's on their records now.

Q Did they know you'd been in trouble before?

A They asked me if I had been so I told them because I knew they could find out anyway. When they looked up my record they saw I hadn't been charged or gone to court. Again they told me to come back in a month's time. During that time I wrote a letter to the company whose board I'd graffitied, apologising, and also a letter to the police officer at the station saying I was sorry.

Q Did that have any effect?

A I think it did because again they said they weren't taking further action and they gave me another caution. But they made it very plain that I was risking getting charged and then I would have a criminal record. They told me I was lucky this time.

Q What was your mother's reaction?

A She thought I was doing graffiti in illegal places because I got a rush from knowing I was doing something I shouldn't, but that's not true with me.

On the other hand, I do know there are graffers out there who live in a messed-up world and they get into crime as well - the graffiti is just one more way they break the law.

Q So did being caught and cautioned make you change your behaviour?

A Yes. I now try to find places I can do graffiti art without getting into trouble. For example, a local greengrocer agreed to let me paint the roll-down blind on

their shop. I did that with friends and it was good fun. Now I do graffiti style painting on canvases. It's not as good as a big surface but I am very aware I can't afford to get in trouble with the police again. ■

> " Now I do graffiti style painting on canvases. "

Talking Points

◆ Do you think that graffiti is a good way for artistic young people to express themselves? Does it improve the appearance of urban environments?

◆ Greg tried to choose abandoned and unwanted buildings to create his graffiti. This is still illegal. Do you think this should be a prosecutable offence? Why?

◆ Each time Greg was let off with a caution. Why do you think the police took this action? Was it the best way?

◆ How do you think graffiti artists should be treated in general?

It Happened to Tom

Tom was attacked by a group of young offenders as he was crossing Hungerford Bridge in London after working late. Although the attack happened two years ago it still affects him.

Q Young men have the highest risk of being victims of street crime and attack. Have you ever worried about it?

A It had never occurred to me to feel worried. I like people and assume they will like me. I just didn't see being a victim of assault as something that would happen to me and it hadn't ever happened before.

Q So what occurred that night?

A It was about 10 p.m. and I had finished work at the film company where I am a runner. I was walking across Hungerford Bridge aiming for Waterloo Station. It was fairly busy; there were several other people walking across it.

Q So what were you doing?

A I was eating a bag of crisps and deep in thought. I heard footsteps coming up alongside me but I didn't think there was anything wrong. I thought someone must want to overtake me so I slowed down to let them pass.

Q So did the person overtake?

A I realised there were several boys behind me. One, who was wearing a hood, passed me and then stood in my path stopping me going forward. I stopped and it was then I realised there were about 15 of these boys aged, I would guess, between 14 and 17. They were all black. When I saw how many there were and they weren't smiling or being friendly I did feel slight panic rising.

> **" I like people and assume they will like me. I just didn't see being a victim of assault as something that would happen to me."**

It's a Fact that...

Just under 13 per cent of cautions or convictions in England and Wales of young offenders relate to violence against the person, while in South Australia the figure is just under 11 per cent.

Q What did they do then?

A The largest of them said, 'Have you got any crisps for my men?' He was talking in a kind of slang. I answered, 'Oh no, sorry, I haven't.' Then a second one said, 'Have you got £5 for me?' So I told him I didn't. Another one put his hand into the pocket of the big coat I was wearing. I remember reacting then and closing my pocket with my hand and I pushed him away. It wasn't a hard push, not aggressive, and I made eye contact with him. I tried to look imploring. I hoped then he would be reasonable.

Q Did that have any effect?

A No. The big guy stepped forward then and told me, 'Don't push my friend.' He punched me in the side of the head. It was a glancing blow and it shocked rather than hurt me. But then the guy next to him hit me and that was a really good punch. I remember he had a ring on.

Q Did that hurt you?

A Yes it did and I remember my legs giving way and I slumped against the bridge wall. I kept remembering at that moment how two young people got thrown over the same bridge the year before and I was thinking, 'Please, I don't want to go over.' I was really scared by this time because it was clear these guys didn't care about me at all.

Q Did anyone come to help you?

A No. I looked at one person passing, hoping they would stop and help but they didn't take any notice of what

41

> "...I remember my legs giving way and I slumped against the bridge wall. I kept remembering at that moment how two young people got thrown over the same bridge the year before."

was happening. I remember feeling angry about that. But then one of the group kicked me in the face and walked on. The others followed, one after the other, kicking my head. I remember seeing the blood spurting out as one after the other kicked me. It all seemed to be happening far away.

Q Were you in a lot of pain?

A Not at that time and, the curious thing was, once the gang had walked on I felt energised and I got up.

Q Were the boys still around?

A They had walked on along the bridge but they were standing there looking at me so I decided to walk the other way. Then the fear just rose up in me and I started running. There were two black girls on the bridge and as I got to them I asked them to help me but they both laughed and swore at me and I saw them going to join the gang who had attacked me.

> **"I wanted to know if anyone who had seen the incident on the bridge had rung the police, but they hadn't. That really upset me, realising that nobody cared that I was being beaten up."**

It's a Fact that...

Only 50 per cent of criminal offences are reported to the police.

Q Did you go for help then?

A I ran to the train station and I saw the look of horror on the guards' faces. They took me to the back room and there was a mirror but I remember not wanting to look in it. I asked one of the guards 'Is my face okay?' But he didn't answer. Someone put a tissue on my nose but I can't remember what they said to me.

Q Did anyone call the police?

A I wasn't aware of it but suddenly a woman police officer was there and she told me there had been a mugging there before. They were going to check the CCTV to see if they could identify anyone. I wanted to know if anyone who had seen the incident on the bridge had rung the police, but they hadn't. That really upset me, realising that nobody cared that I was being beaten up. That's been a big part of not feeling safe since.

Q What happened then?

A I was taken to hospital. I started feeling very worried about my teeth falling out and the state of my face. I was offered a mirror to look in and this time I accepted but I held the nurse's hand while I looked. I had a huge bump on my nose, which was broken, a very fat lip and a half-closed eye.

Q In the following days what did you feel about the attack?

A I thought a lot about the guys who attacked me, and why they had done it. They didn't take my bag or steal anything and in a way that made it worse, much more personal. I wanted to believe they would feel bad but the police said they doubted they would feel any remorse. Rather they would be laughing with their friends about it. That felt really terrible. It was very hard to accept that I was nothing to them but that they had had such an effect on my life.

43

have liked to see them go to prison, but the police doubted they would catch them because they probably weren't from the area. And they never did.

Q Were there other feelings?

A I felt I was a coward, a pushover, ashamed of myself. It's that male thing: I felt I should have been able to fight back and stand up for myself even though logically I can see that you can't with a big gang of strong people all at you. But I had fantasies later that were classic symptoms of post-traumatic stress disorder, where I would re-enact the scene in my mind and I would do things differently and beat the attackers. This went on for months.

Q Did you get any psychological help?

A I was offered counselling but I didn't go. I wanted to deal with it myself.

Q Was there anything you did that really helped?

A I decided I must force myself to go to a black

> **"I felt I was a coward, a pushover, ashamed of myself."**

Q Did you feel any desire for revenge?

A I thought about the boys a lot and I felt hate. Real hate. And I had a fantasy about having a little zapper thing, which I could use to throw them over the bridge and kill them. They were never caught but I would very much have liked them prosecuted. In fact I'd

country and see if I could cope because I was feeling very fearful of black males. So I went, by myself, to Papua New Guinea. I was terrified the first day but everyone was immensely friendly and kind. A family invited me to go and stay in a village with them. The fact that it was a completely different culture made a big difference. It was actually a healing experience.

Q So are you completely over it?

A Well, that's the awful thing. It happened two years ago but I am still aware that it's affecting me. The thing that upsets me quite a lot is that it has made me a bit racist and I never was before. I live in a very black neighbourhood and have always felt at ease there and been part of the community and I had black friends at college. But now if I see a group of black boys or young men at night I can't deal with it. I don't want to be this way, it makes me feel wretched. However, a black guy has just started at the film company where I work and the fact that we get on well and he likes me makes me feel better.

Q Otherwise you are back to normal?

A No. I live with a completely different view of myself since the incident happened. Now I feel I am an obvious victim, a target people will choose to pick on. My confidence has gone right down. I think I'll always believe that gang picked on me because of who I am, not just because I was unlucky enough to be in the wrong place at the wrong time. ■

> **"I live with a completely different view of myself since the incident happened. Now I feel I am an obvious victim..."**

Talking Points

◆ Attacks by young offenders are more common in gangs, as in this case, than for older offenders. Why do you think this is? What do such gangs offer young people?

◆ Tom believes he was attacked because he is a 'victim'. Are some people natural victims or not? If so, what makes them this way and what could they do to prevent this?

◆ This was a brutal and unprovoked attack. Had the young offenders been caught, however, they would have been treated differently to offenders over 18. Do you think this is fair? At what age do you think we are aware of right and wrong and when should we become legally responsible for our actions?

Useful addresses and contacts

UK

RPS Rainer
A charity offering support for 10- to 25-year-olds who are at risk from offending, as well as family breakdown or homelessness.

Rectory Lodge
High Street
Brasted
Westerham
Kent
TN16 1JF
Tel: 01959 578200
Fax: 01959 561891
www.rpsrainer.org

Youth Justice Board
Aims to prevent offending by children and young people.

11 Carteret Street
London SW1H 9DL
Tel: 020 7271 3033
www.youth-justice-board.gov.uk

www.thesite.org.uk
Features advice on youth centres near you.

Youth Access
Local youth advisory services. For the nearest one, contact:

1-2 Taylors Yard
67 Alderbrook Road
London
SW12 8AD
Tel: 020 8772 9900 (Office)

Victim Support
Charity offering support and information to all victims of crime, except theft of, or from, cars and child abuse in the family.

National Office:
Cranmer House, 39 Brixton Road, London SW9 6DZ

Tel: 020 7735 9166
Helpline: 0845 3030 900

www.victimsupport.org.uk

National Drugs Helpline
A 24-hour freephone number for queries or concerns regarding drugs.

0800 776600

AUSTRALIA

National Children's and Youth Law Centre

An independent non-profit organisation working for all Australians under the age of 25. They provide advice and information about legal rights and responsibilities.

Postal address:
National Children's and Youth Law Centre
C/- University of NSW
Sydney NSW 2052

Street address:
32 Botany Street
Randwick NSW 2031

Telephone: (02) 9398 7488

Their website 'lawstuff', aimed at young people, has information on the law in every Australian state:

www.lawstuff.org.au

Note to parents and teachers: Every effort has been made by the Publishers to ensure that these websites are suitable for teenagers, that they are of the highest educational value, and that they contain no inappropriate or offensive material. However, because of the nature of the Internet, it is impossible to guarantee that the contents of these sites will not be altered. We strongly advise that Internet access is supervised by a responsible adult.

Glossary

amphetamines
An illegal stimulant drug that comes in powder or tablet form.

assault
A violent physical or verbal attack.

bail
Money that is required as security for the temporary release of an offender while he or she waits for their trial. Serious offenders will not be offered bail.

bedsit
Accommodation with a combined bedroom, living room and cooking area.

bind over
To order a person to do something such as to keep the peace (not cause any trouble).

caution
A formal legal warning for an offence.

Children's Court Clinic (especially Australia)
Where under-age drug offenders go to be assessed for psychological, clinical or other therapy after they have entered the Children's Court.

conditional discharge
An order made by a criminal court where an offender will not be sentenced unless a further offence is committed within a set period.

custodial sentence
The decision of a court of law to commit a person to a set time of imprisonment.

good behaviour bond
When a person's freedom depends on their behaviour. If they re-offend, they may be sentenced.

hip hop
A style of pop music of US black origin, featuring rap. Graffiti is associated with hip hop music.

income support
Money given by the government to people who are unemployed, sick or on low pay.

magistrate
An official person who conducts a court for minor cases.

pathological
Something caused by a physical or mental disorder.

post-traumatic stress
A condition of emotional strain after an injury or severe shock.

probation
A system of supervising and monitoring offenders, instead of, or after, sending them to prison.

rights
A set of legal rules to ensure somone who is arrested is treated fairly, for example - the right to request legal representation (such as a solicitor).

solicitor
A person who can advise young offenders on the law and their situation.

sentence
A decision by a court of law, especially a punishment such as a term in prison, given to a person convicted in a criminal trial.

speed
A type of amphetamine.

substance abuse
When a person takes drugs, often illegally, and puts their health at risk.

twocking
A slang term for taking a car without the consent of the owner.

Index

assault 15, 30, 40-45

caution, 4, 14, 15, 38, 39, 41, 47
community order 4, 6, 10
court 8, 13, 14, 16, 21, 23, 24, 29, 30, 33, 47
crime 4, 5, 11, 37, 39
    car 5, 10, 12, 16, 17, 21, 22, 24, 25, 27, 28, 29, 30, 33, 47
    robbery 8, 16, 19, 25, 29, 30
    street, 6, 7, 8, 9, 40

counselling 29, 33, 44

drug abuse 28, 29, 30, 32, 33, 47

graffiti 34-39, 47

influence of friends 4, 5, 7, 11, 14, 16, 18, 20, 21, 22, 23, 24, 26, 27

law, the 4, 6, 14, 33, 38, 39, 47

mugging 24, 25, 27, 43

parents, role of 4, 11, 12-16, 18, 22, 23, 27, 31

police 9, 12, 13, 14, 15, 22, 23, 28, 34, 37, 38, 39, 43, 44
prison 6, 9, 10, 11, 16, 19, 20, 21, 25, 27, 44, 47
probation 12, 17, 18, 20, 23, 24, 47

racism 7, 9, 45
RPS Rainer Fresh Start project 12, 17, 19, 46

school 6, 7, 13, 15, 20, 21, 22, 24, 29, 30, 34
secure unit 20, 24, 25, 27
supervision order 8, 20, 24, 25

victim 5, 11, 27, 33, 40-45, 46

warning 4, 22, 23, 27

Getting active!

On your own:
Conduct a survey to find out how worried people are about youth crime. You might want to ask them to compare their concerns about crime with other national issues such as health or education.

In pairs:
Do some research into the law on young offenders. When is a child legally responsible? What happens in court? What kind of sentences are used for different crimes? Make a simple booklet that would help a young offender understand the system.

In groups:
Organise a debate on a crime-related topic of your choice, for example, 'Parents should take full responsibility for the actions of children under 16' or 'Prison sentences do not work as a deterrent to crime' etc. Organise people to take both sides of the argument and conclude with an audience vote on the issue.